P9-EAI-918

THE PORTABLE 7 HABITS™

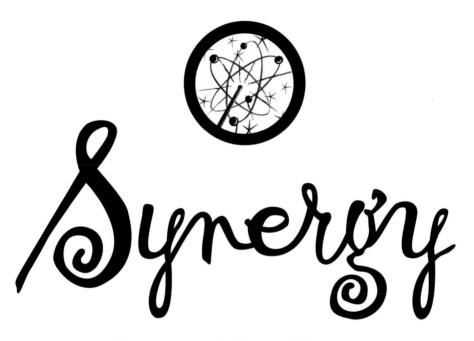

Synergy

Connecting to the Power of Cooperation

THE 7 HABITS
OF HIGHLY EFFECTIVE PEOPLE®

Other Portable 7 Habits Books
Choice: Choosing the Proactive Life You Want to Live
Vision: Defining Your Destiny in Life
Purpose: Focusing on What Matters Most
Abundance: Fulfilling Your Potential for Success
Trust: Sharing Ideas, Insights, and Understanding
Renewal: Nourishing Body, Mind, Heart, and Soul

Other Books from Franklin Covey
The 7 Habits of Highly Effective People
The 7 Habits of Highly Effective Families
The 7 Habits of Highly Effective Teens
The 7 Habits of Highly Effective Teens Journal
Daily Reflections for Highly Effective Teens
Daily Reflections for Highly Effective People
Living the 7 Habits

Loving Reminders for Kids
Loving Reminders for Couples
Loving Reminders for Families
Loving Reminders Teen to Teen
Loving Reminders to Make Kids Laugh
Quotes and Quips

Franklin Covey
2200 West Parkway Boulevard
Salt Lake City, Utah 84119-2099

Concept: Cheryl Kerzner
Design: Jenny Peterson
Illustration: Tammy Smith
Written and compiled by Debra Harris
Contributors: John Crowley, Ann Hobson, Sunny Larson, Shelley Orgill

Manufactured in United States of America

ISBN 1-929494-14-9

CONTENTS

All things are connected. Whatever befalls the earth befalls the sons of the earth. Man did not weave the web of life. He is merely a strand on it. Whatever he does to the web he does to himself.

—CHIEF SEATTLE

INTRODUCTION

Creating a global society that comes together synergistically means respecting the strength and power of diversity. It means becoming more culturally savvy to function more effectively with people who are different. All it takes is mutual acceptance to work from a deeper place of respect, honor, and integrity.

In *Synergy: Connecting to the Power of Cooperation*, we've simplified the powerful principles behind *The 7 Habits of Highly Effective People* by Stephen R. Covey to allow you to enhance your communication and people skills to find common ground for all concerned.

There are no roadmaps to follow. No instructions. No how-tos. And no formulas for success. Instead you'll find a collection of contemporary quotes, thought-provoking questions, provocative messages, and practical wisdom in an easy-to-read format.

As you turn these pages, take the words of advice to heart, mind, body, and soul. Think about what you read. Ponder how and what it would take to benefit from the creative potency that different viewpoints and lifestyles can bring. Let the wisdom inspire you to play an active role in creating a society where differences are honored, diversity is treasured, and the human spirit is lifted.

In essence, make it a habit to synergize.

HABIT 6: SYNERGIZE®

Work together to achieve more.

AWARENESS

The person who is truly effective has the humility and reverence to recognize his own perceptual limitations and to appreciate the rich resources available through interaction with the hearts and minds of other human beings.

——STEPHEN R. COVEY, *The 7 Habits of Highly Effective People*

When you learn
to live for others,
they will learn to
live for you.

—PARAMAHANSA YOGANANDA

SHOW UP

and choose to be present.

Do not judge strangers harshly.

Remember that **every stranger you meet is you.**

—SIDNEY SHELDON

The only way to get through talking with people that you don't really have anything in common with is to pretend you're hosting your own little talk show. This is what I do. You pretend there's a little desk around you. There's a little chair over there and you can interview them. The only problem with this is there's no way you can say, "Hey, it's been great having you on the show, but I'm afraid we're out of time."

—JERRY SEINFELD

We are the people, our parents warned us about.

—JIMMY BUFFETT

Know your own failings, passions, and prejudices

so you can separate them from what you see. Know also when you actually have thought through to the nature of the thing with which you are dealing and when you are not thinking at all...Knowing yourself and knowing the facts, you can judge whether you can change the situation so it is more to your liking. If you cannot—or if you do not know how to improve on things—then discipline yourself to the adjustments that will be necessary.

—BERNARD BARUCH

M

any of the truths we
cling to are greatly
the result of our
own point of view.

ARE YOU AWARE?

◎ **Become more aware of how other people live.**
Look at it as a learning experience. Don't let someone else's lifestyle or way of doing things bother you just because it's not how you would do it.

◎ **Be yourself at all times.**
You can't be phony if you want to work well with others. They'll see through you like you're wearing cellophane.

◎ **Control negativity.**
Try to see another point of view. Not every problem is actually a problem. Most are really an opportunity in disguise. So keep your eyes open.

◎ **Stay in the present.**
Forget about what others may have done to you in the past. Let go of any blame or resentment. It's not worth hanging on to if you want to establish any kind of synergy in the present.

◎ **When someone makes you angry, don't respond with a personal attack.**
The worst thing you can do is attack someone else in front of a group. Either talk to the person privately later when you're calmer or chalk it up to his or her own problem.

◎ **Work on your awareness every day.**
You have to constantly work at being aware. Be more accepting of people's contributions. You don't have all the answers so don't expect others to have them.

HATING PEOPLE

is like burning down your own house to get rid of a rat.

—HARRY EMERSON FOSDICK

I was doing a show on victims confronting their criminals. A 17-year-old girl was on the air speaking to the man who, four years earlier, had beaten her beyond recognition and left her for dead. She'd had 17 surgeries and complete facial reconstruction. She said to him, "I don't hate you. I hate what you did to me. And I have had to learn to forgive you so I could go on with my own life." To this day it is the most powerful thing I've ever seen. In that moment, she expressed why we're here—to learn to live in spite of the human condition, to **transcend the human condition of being fearful.** We get so bogged down in worldly things we don't understand that we're here for a spiritual quest. Understanding that this is a journey is the most exciting part of being human. It has revolutionized my life.

—OPRAH WINFREY

Your mind works best when it's open.

DIVERSITY

The person who is truly effective values the differences because those differences add to his knowledge, to his understanding of reality. When we're left to our own experiences, we constantly suffer from a shortage of data.

—STEPHEN R. COVEY, *The 7 Habits of Highly Effective People*

GREETINGS

I am pleased to see that we are different. May we together become greater than the sum of both of us.

—MR. SPOCK

I once complained to my father that I didn't seem to

be able to do things the same way other people did.

Dad's advice? "Margo,

DON'T BE A SHEEP.

People hate sheep. They eat sheep."

—MARGO KAUFMAN

*E*verything that irritates us about others can lead us to an understanding of ourselves. Always put yourself in others' shoes.

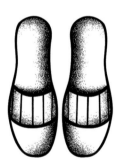

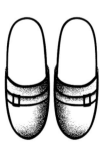

You need to know
that you can be
totally yourself
and still belong.

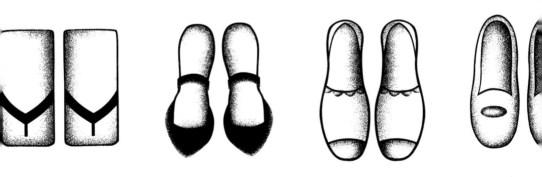

It's a bittersweet symphony, that's **LIFE.**

—THE VERVE

SHARE THE SIMILARITIES

celebrate

THE DIFFERENCES

—M. SCOTT PECK

You clones are all alike.

—©ASHLEIGH BRILLIANT

THE TURTLE TEST

One of the most important people for you to observe and know inside out is you. Most of us experience moments of "turtle behavior." When we're confronted with an opportunity to learn information that challenges what we think we know, we choose to pull back into our self-satisfied shells. Take the quiz below and see what your "turtle rating" is. Rate each statement from **1 to 5**, according to how true it is of you (**1 = almost never, 3 = sometimes, 5 = almost always**).

_____ When someone contradicts me, my first reaction is to argue.

_____ I tend to make up my mind quickly.

_____ When someone asks me a question, I often sound more sure of the answer than I actually am.

_____ I'd rather win than be right.

_____ I know as much or more than most people I hang around with.

_____ Once I've made up my mind about something, I rarely change it.

_____ When I know I'm mistaken, I find it difficult to admit it.

_____ I spend as little time as possible with people who are smarter than me.

_____ I like talking better than listening.

_____ I consider my education complete.

Add up your score. If you rated **10 to 15**, you're on the right track. Keep going. If you scored **16 to 35**, you need to pay more attention to your "turtle" habits and find ways to change them. If you're in the **36 to 50** range, you're about to be inducted into the "Know-It-All Club" of boors and bullies. Time for some humility, soul-searching, and a major overhaul of your learning style. Become one of the ones who gets it!

——PHILLIP C. MCGRAW

Racism isn't born, folks, it's taught. I have a two-year-old son. You know what he hates? **Naps!** End of list.

——DENIS LEARY

We will have to repent in this generation not merely for the hateful words and actions of the bad people but for the appalling silence of the good people.

—MARTIN LUTHER KING JR.

Why is it always easier to dislike something than it is to understand it?

ACCEPTANCE

You can be synergistic within yourself even in the midst of a very adversarial environment. You don't have to take insults personally. You can sidestep negative energy; you can look for the good in others and utilize that good, as different as it may be, to improve your point of view, and to enlarge your perspective.

——STEPHEN R. COVEY, *The 7 Habits of Highly Effective People*

Acceptance is not submission;

it is acknowledgement of the facts of the situation.

Then deciding what you're going to do about it.

—KATHLEEN CASEY THEISEN

YOU
cannot
see eye to eye
with those you
look down
upon.

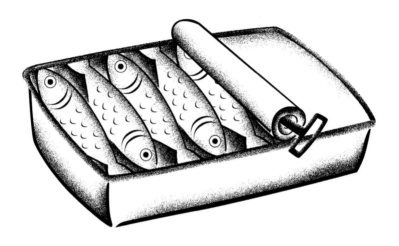

I know I'm an acquired taste: I'm anchovies. And not everyone wants those hairy little things. If I was potato chips, I could go more places.

—TORI AMOS

The art of acceptance

is the art of making someone who

has just done you a small favor

wish that he might have done you

a greater one.

—RUSSELL LYNES

CAN YOU JUST ACCEPT WHAT IS?

Your new coworker's idea was chosen by the boss.
You think: That little brown-noser. I'm going to make her life miserable.
Replace it with: I have to admit that it was a good idea. I'll be more open to her suggestions next time.

The person you're dating wants some space.
You think: You're lying. You're just out bobbing-for-supermodels again.
Replace it with: Fine. I've got a life. If it's supposed to work out, it will.

Your best friend gently points out one of your flaws.
You think: Oh, as if you're so perfect.
Replace with: I know I do that. I need to work on it. Thank you.

A person from a different culture moves in next door.
You think: They're way too different. We'd have nothing in common.
Replace it with: They look interesting. I'll go introduce myself.

Accepting what is doesn't mean you have to ignore the possibilities that exist. It just means you might surprise yourself by trying a different perspective once in awhile

Expecting the world to treat you fairly because

you are a good person is a little like expecting

the bull not to attack you because you are

a vegetarian.

—DENNIS WHOLEY

THOSE WHO CAN,

DO.

THOSE WHO CAN'T, CRITICIZE.

In every community there is work to be done…

In every heart there is the power to do it.

—MARIANNE WILLIAMSON

Love

is the willingness to accept another person with all of his or her faults and limitations, and to be infinitely grateful that this other person accepts you with all of yours.

—HAROLD S. KUSHNER

If people don't **measure up** to your standards,

perhaps you should **check your yardstick.**

One day our descendants will think it incredible that we paid so much attention to things like the amount of melanin in our skin or the shape of our eyes or our gender instead of the unique identities of each of us as complex human beings.

—FRANKLIN THOMAS

APPRECIATION

Achieving unity—oneness—with ourselves, with our loved ones, with our friends and working associates, is the most delicious fruit of the 7 Habits. Most of us have tasted this fruit of true unity from time to time in the past, as we have also tasted the bitter, lonely fruit of disunity—and we know how precious and fragile unity is.

—STEPHEN R. COVEY, *The 7 Habits of Highly Effective People*

Don't be in a hurry to condemn because he doesn't do what you do or think as you think or as fast. There was a time when you didn't know what you know today.

—MALCOLM X

To work in the world lovingly

means that we are defining what we will be **for,** rather than reacting
to what we are **against.**

—CHRISTINA BALDWIN

Our belief in one another

is what unites

us and encourages us to

Be Our Best.

—SARAH MCLACHLAN

THE
ULTIMATE
MEASURE OF A MAN

is not where he stands in moments of

comfort, but where he stands at times

of challenge and controversy.

—MARTIN LUTHER KING JR.

CAN YOU RELATE?

Answer the following questions true or false. Think about specific instances in your life before answering.

_____ I demand perfection from myself and everyone around me.

_____ I am surprised when others don't like me or my ideas.

_____ People continually make promises to me without following through.

_____ I don't have many friends who I really like or trust.

_____ I get tired of all this political correctness. I don't have to like everyone.

_____ I don't appreciate other people's opinions of me.

_____ I don't like change.

_____ I work better alone than in groups.

_____ I tend be more negative than positive.

_____ I'm afraid people will find out that I'm not what I appear.

If the majority of your answers are true, it's time to turn off the negativity tapes and rid yourself of your limited beliefs. In order to know yourself, you have to understand the lives and actions of others. Be a student of human nature and appreciate what everyone can bring to the party. If the majority of your answers are false, you're comfortable with yourself and how you relate to people of all kinds. You're a student of life and know learning from others helps you in your own life.

I've learned...

that sometimes the

people you expect to

kick you when you're

down will be the ones to

help you get back up.

—UNKNOWN

So many of the negative conclusions we've drawn about life are erroneous, foolish and exaggerated.

It is probably not true, for example, that the whole world is out to get you at any given time. (At any given time, only 20 percent of the world is out to get you. The rest of the world has your mailing address, just in case.)

—STEPHANIE BRUSH

We are not put on this earth for ourselves, but are placed here for each other. If you are there always for others, then in time of need, someone will be there for you.

—JEFF WARNER

If you judge others you will have no time to love them.

—MOTHER TERESA

INTEGRATION

Synergy means that the whole is greater than the sum of its parts. It means that the relationship that the parts have to each other is a part in and of itself. It is not only a part, but the most catalytic, empowering, unifying, and exciting part.

——STEPHEN R. COVEY, *The 7 Habits of Highly Effective People*

*N*ever look down on anybody unless you're helping him up.

—JESSE JACKSON

Life
works **best**
when **you** choose
what you
got.

—UNKNOWN

I've learned...

that your family won't always be there for you. It may seem funny, but people you aren't related to can take care of you and love you and teach you to trust people again. Families aren't biological.

—UNKNOWN

REAL SISTERHOOD

is a bunch of dames in bathrobes throwing back M&Ms and making each other laugh.

—MAXINE WILKIE

Beginning today,

treat everyone you meet as if

they were going to be dead by midnight.

Extend to them all the care, kindness,

and understanding you can muster,

and do it with no thought of any reward.

Your life will never be the same again.

—OG MANDINO

Cooperation
can be spelled
with two letters:
WE.

People who upset us the most are our best teachers.

I am of the opinion that my life belongs to the whole community

and as long as I live, it is my privilege to do for it whatever

I can. I want to be thoroughly used up when I die, for the

harder I work the more I live. I rejoice in life

for its own sake. Life is no brief candle to me.

It is a splendid torch

which I have got hold of for the moment,

and I want to make it burn as brightly

as possible before handing it on to

future generations.

—GEORGE BERNARD SHAW

...fear makes strangers of people who should be friends.

—SHIRLEY MACLAINE

COLLABORATION

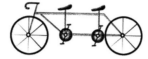

The more genuine the involvement, the more sincere and sustained the participation in analyzing and solving problems, the greater the release of everyone's creativity and of their commitment to what they create.

——STEPHEN R. COVEY, *The 7 Habits of Highly Effective People*

What is exciting is not for one person to be stronger than the other…but for two people to have met their match and yet they are equally as stubborn, as obstinate, as passionate, as crazy as the other.

—BARBRA STREISAND

Curious people ask questions.

DETERMINED PEOPLE FIND THE ANSWERS.

Call it a **clan**, call it a **network**, call it a **tribe**, call it a **family.** Whatever you call it, whoever you are, **you need one.**

—JANE HOWARD

EVERYONE'S ENTITLED TO OPINIONS.

But don't abuse your privilege.

ONE WAY

is not the only way

Remember,

we all stumble, every one of us.
That's why it's a comfort to go
hand in hand.

—EMILY KIMBROUGH

Combining everyone's **KNOWLEDGE BEGETS MORE KNOWLEDGE,** the way combining rice and beans begets more protein.

—ELIZABETH HILTS

NOTHING
is impossible

as long as you don't
have to do it yourself.

Synergy
is exciting.
Creativity
is exciting.

It's phenomenal what openness and

communication can produce. The

possibilities of truly significant gain,

of significant improvement are so

real that it's worth the risk such

openness entails.

—STEPHEN R. COVEY

Great minds
DON'T
think alike,

for that is why they are great.

——DEREK WEIDL

Do you play well with others?

It's very reassuring and spiritual to be connected with something

larger than yourself and the inside of your own head.

—JOAN OSBORNE

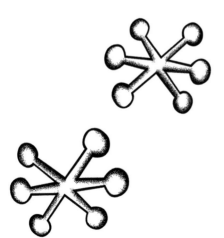

We're souls having a human experience.

—BRIAN WEISS

INNOVATION

Ineffective people live day after day with unused potential. They experience synergy only in small, peripheral ways in their lives. But creative experiences can be produced regularly, consistently, almost daily in people's lives. It requires enormous personal security and openness and a spirit of adventure.

—STEPHEN R. COVEY, *The 7 Habits of Highly Effective People*

To live a creative life, we must
lose our fear
of being wrong.

—JOSEPH CHILTON PIERCE

Those persons are happiest in this restless and mutable world who are in **love** with change, who **delight** in what is new simply because it differs from what is old; who **rejoice** in every innovation, and find a strange alert **pleasure** in all that is, and that has never been before.

—AGNES REPPLIER

I dream for a Living.

—STEVEN SPIELBERG

Don't ask, "What if it doesn't work?" Ask instead, "What if it does?

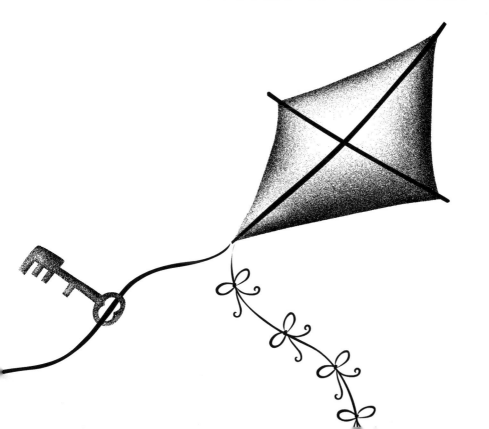

I've learned...

that heroes are the people
who do what has to be
done when it needs to
be done, regardless of
the consequences.

—UNKNOWN

INNOVATION

is the best way to short-circuit the status quo.

But the fact that some geniuses were laughed at does not imply that all who are laughed at are geniuses. They laughed at Columbus, they laughed at Fulton, they laughed at the Wright brothers. But they also laughed at Bozo the Clown

—CARL SAGAN

TEAMWORK:
MORE THAN A FEW GOOD IDEAS.

A good idea can come from anywhere and anyone at any time.

To be brilliant don't worry about feeling stupid along the way.

Allow diversity to stimulate creativity.

Most great ideas are combined and worked with before they're successful.

Forget the rules. There are no rules in innovation.

Don't get too stuck on your own ideas. Allow them to grow through input.

Group-think. Let everyone throw their ideas into the mix.

Be a piece to the puzzle not the entire solution.

Trust your team and their feedback.

Remember, teams can accomplish what an individual cannot.

Originality has nothing to do with priority…just
because someone used G-minor before doesn't
make Mozart a copycat.

—STEPHEN MITCHELL

Shake the Etch-A-Sketch in your head, start over constantly, and come at the problem from wildly different angles. **Don't keep sniffing the same fire hydrant.** Run through the entire neighborhood.

—LUKE SULLIVAN

You say I'm a dreamer, but I'm not the only one.

—JOHN LENNON

SYNERGY

The essence of synergy is to value differences—to respect them, to build on strengths, to compensate for weaknesses…Once people have experienced real synergy, they are never quite the same again. They know the possibility of having other such mind-expanding adventures in the future.

—STEPHEN R. COVEY, *The 7 Habits of Highly Effective People*

$\mathcal{T}$he true wonder of the world is available everywhere, in the minutest parts of our bodies, in the vast expanses of the cosmos, and in the interconnectedness of these and all things.

—MICHAEL STARK

When you blame others you give up a perfect opportunity to change.

SYNERGY'S A-LIST

HAVE A HEALTHY RESPECT FOR DIVERSITY.
Everyone is unique and original just like you.

BE ABLE TO RELAX AROUND OTHERS.
Being wound too tight is for watches.

VALUE OPINIONS WHETHER YOU AGREE OR NOT.
Leave "My Way" to Frank.

CREATE BALANCE.
The idea is to give and take without being piggy about it.

BE RESPONSIVE TO NEW IDEAS.
No mind-closure allowed.

DEVELOP TRUST.
Tough right out of the chute but worth it in the end.

DISCOVER AND SHARE COMMON INTERESTS.
Go out of your way to mind-meld often.

HUMOR.
Never leave home without it.

DON'T STEREOTYPE.
You'll be wrong 100% of the time.

BE REAL.
Enough said.

F

act of the matter is, there is no hip world, there is no straight world. There's a world, you see, which has people in it who believe in a variety of different things. Everybody believes in something and everybody, by virtue of the fact that they believe in something, uses that something to support their own existence.

—FRANK ZAPPA

COMING TOGETHER

is a beginning;

KEEPING TOGETHER

is progress;

WORKING TOGETHER

is success.

The only reason we don't open our hearts and minds to other people is that they trigger confusion in us that we don't feel brave enough or sane enough to deal with. To the degree that we look clearly and compassionately at ourselves, we feel confident and fearless about looking into someone else's eyes.

—PEMA CHÖDRÖN

The man who follows the crowd

will usually get no further than

the crowd. **The man who**

walks alone is likely

to find himself in places

no one has ever been.

——ALAN ASHLEY-PITTS

The people with whom we have contact are the chisels and hammers that craft what we will become. Our life's journey is an ever-unfolding work of art that tells the story of where we have been and with whom we have traveled.

—IYANLA VAN ZANT

The trouble with most people is their trouble with most people.

ACCOMPLISHMENT

Like the Far Eastern philosophy, "We seek not to imitate the masters, rather we seek what they sought," we seek not to imitate past creative synergistic experiences; rather we seek new ones around new and different and sometimes higher purposes.

——STEPHEN R. COVEY, *The 7 Habits of Highly Effective People*

At first people refuse to believe that a strange new thing can be done, then they begin to hope it can be done, then they see it can be done—then it is done and all the world wonders why it was not done centuries ago.

—FRANCES HODGSON BURNETT

There is no reason to feel diagonally parked
in a parallel universe.
ENJOY BEING DIAGONAL.
Besides, parallel parking can be a pain in the neck.

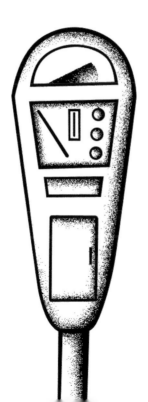

*Y*ou decide to do something, perform one small action, and suddenly it's a tide, the momentum is going, and there's no possibility of turning back. Somehow, even though you thought you foresaw all that would happen, you didn't know the pace would pick up so.

—AMANDA CROSS

Don't worry over what other people are thinking about you.

They're too busy worrying over what you are thinking about them. If one dream should fall and break into a thousand pieces, never be afraid to pick one of those pieces up and begin again.

—FLAVIA WEEDN

THE ONLY THING TO LEARN FROM
GOING BY THE BOOK
IS THAT YOU'RE
GOING BY THE BOOK.

I've learned...

that our background and circumstances may have influenced who we are, but we are responsible for who we become.

—UNKNOWN

MONEY

is what people without talent use to keep score.

——JEREMY C. EPWORTH

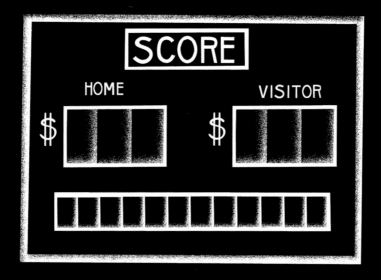

The way is long—Let us get together.

The way is difficult—let us help each other.

The way is joyful—let us share it.

The way is ours alone—let us go in love.

The way grows before us—let us begin.

—ZEN INVOCATION

It's easy to make a buck. It's a lot tougher to make a difference.

—TOM BROKAW

TRANSFORMATION

Could synergy not create a new script for the next generation—one that is more geared to service and contribution, and is less protective, less adversarial, less selfish; one that is more open, more trusting, more giving, and is less defensive, protective, and political; one that is more loving, more caring, and is less possessive and judgmental?

——STEPHEN R. COVEY, *The 7 Habits of Highly Effective People*

You say you want a revolution, Well you know, we all want to change the world.

—PAUL MCCARTNEY
AND JOHN LENNON

Just when the caterpillar thought the world was over, it became a butterfly.

—UNKNOWN

If you don't think one person can make

a difference, consider what one cigar

can do to a crowded restaurant.

Transcendence is the power to be born anew, to make a fresh start, to turn over a new leaf, to begin with a clean slate, to enter into a state of grace, to have a second chance...because transcendence is an ever-new state of being, once you enter into it, each new moment is alive with fresh possibilities that may never have seemed possible before.

—ROBERT FRITZ

There's only now,

there's only here.

Give into love,

or live in fear.

No other path,

no other way,

no day but

TODAY.

—*RENT*

Only in **growth, reform, and change,** paradoxically enough, is true security to be found.

—ANNE MORROW LINDBERGH

I am not the same,

having seen the moon shine on the other side of the world.

—MARYANNE RADMACHER-HERSHEY

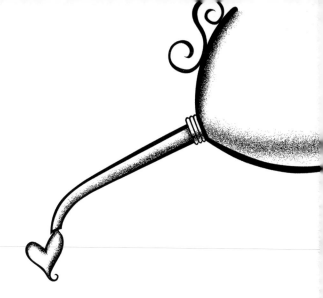

Kindness is the oil that takes the friction out of life.

So often we think we have got to make a difference and be a big dog. Let us just try to be little fleas biting. Enough fleas biting strategically can make a very big dog very uncomfortable.

—MARIAN WRIGHT EDELMAN

Do the right thing.

—SPIKE LEE

About Franklin Covey

Franklin Covey is the world's leading time management and life leadership company. Based on proven principles, our services and products are used by more than 15 million people worldwide. We work with a wide variety of clients, Fortune 500 material, as well as smaller companies, communities, and organizations. You may know us from our world-renowned Franklin Planner or any of our books in the 7 Habits series. By the way, Franklin Covey books have sold over 15 million copies worldwide—over $1\frac{1}{2}$ million each year. But what you may not know about Franklin Covey is we also offer leadership training, motivational workshops, personal coaching, audiotapes and videotapes, and *PRIORITIES* magazine just to name a few.

Let Us Know What You Think

We'd love to hear your suggestions or comments about *Synergy: Connecting to the Power of Cooperation* or any of our Portable 7 Habits books. All seven books in the series will be published in 2000.

www.franklincovey.com/portable7

The Portable 7 Habits
Franklin Covey
MS0733-CK
2200 West Parkway Boulevard
Salt Lake City, Utah 84119-2331 USA

1-800-952-6839
International (801) 229-1333 Fax (801) 229-1233

PERMISSIONS

RECOMMENDED READING

Covey, Stephen R. *The 7 Habits of Highly Effective People*. Simon & Schuster, 1989.

———. *Living the 7 Habits*. Simon & Schuster, 1999.

———. *Principle-Centered Leadership: Strategies for Personal and Professional Leadership*. Simon & Schuster, 1993.

Arrien, Angeles, Rianne Eisler, and Jacqueline Haessly. *Working Together: Producing Synergy by Honoring Diversity*. New Leaders Press, 1998.

Brilliant, Ashleigh. *We've Been through So Much Together and Most of It Was Your Fault*. Woodbridge Press, 1997.

Bucher, Richard D. *Diversity Consciousness: Opening Our Minds to People, Cultures, and Opportunities*. Prentice Hall, 1999.

Campbell, Andrew, and Kathleen Sommers. *Strategic Synergy*. International Thomson Business Press, 1998.

Eli, Quinn. *Many Strong and Beautiful Voices*. Running Press, 1997.

Fritz, Robert. *The Path of Least Resistence*. Fawcett Columbine, 1989.

Graham, Lawrence Otis. *Proversity: Getting Past Face Value and Finding the Soul of People—A Manager's Journey*. John Wiley & Sons, 1997.

Hateley, Barbara J., Warren H. Hateley, and Barbara Schmidt. *A Peacock in the Land of Penguins: A Tale of Diversity and Discovery*. Berrett-Koehler Publishers, 1996.

Hunter, Dale, Anne Bailey, and Bill Taylor. *The Art of Facilitation: How to Create Group Synergy*. Fisher Books, 1995.

Jones, Shirley Ann. *Simply Living: The Spirit of the Indigenous People*. New World Library, 1999.

McGraw, Phillip C. *The Life Strategies Workbook: Exercises and Self-Tests to Help You Change Your Life*. Hyperion, 2000.

Michalski, Walter J., and Dana G. King. *40 Tools for Cross-Functional Teams: Building Synergy for Breakthrough Creativity, Vol. 2*. Productivity Press, 1998.

McAlindon, Harold R. *The Little Book of Big Ideas*. Cumberland House, 1999.

Singer, Madeleine. *Psychology of Synergy: A Guide to Personal Power*. New Falcon, 1991.

Sullivan, Luke. *Hey, Whipple, Squeeze This. A Guide to Creating Great Ads*. John Wiley & Sons, 1998.

Trompenaars, Fons, and Charles Hampden-Turner. *Riding the Waves of Culture: Understanding Cultural Diversity in Global Business*. McGraw-Hill, 1997.

VanZant, Iyanla. *Faith in the Valley*. Simon & Schuster, 1998.